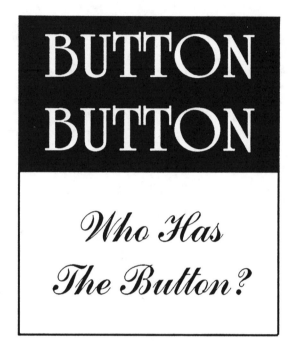

BUTTON
BUTTON

Who Has
The Button?

A Drama About Women's Lives Today

By Ruth Harriet Jacobs, Ph.D.

Other works by Ruth Harriet Jacobs, Ph.D.

Be An Outrageous Older Woman—A RASP (Remarkable Aging
    Smart Person)
We Speak for Peace
Women Who Touched My Life
Out of Their Mouths
Life After Youth: Female, Forty—What Next?
Re-Engagement in Later Life: Re-Employment and Remarriage,
    with Barbara H. Vinick
Older Women Surviving and Thriving: A Manual

Button Button
Who has the Button?

BUTTON BUTTON

Who Has The Button?

A Drama About Women's Lives Today

By Ruth Harriet Jacobs, Ph.D.

Cover Design: Natalie Cederquist—Hummingbird Graphics
Text Design: Robin McArdle
Production: Paradigm Publishing Company

Library of Congress Number: 96-75957
ISBN 1-879198-06-1

First Published in 1983. Second printing in 1988. Third revised printing in 1996 by:

Knowledge, Ideas & Trends, Inc.
1131-0 Tolland Turnpike, Suite 175
Manchester, CT 06040

1-800-826-0529

10 9 8 7 6 5 4 3
Printed in the United States of America

About Performance and Royalties

This poetic drama is for reading to yourself or for reading aloud. It is moving when read aloud from scripts. It does no have to be memorized.

This play may be presented as a whole with an intermission between the two acts or parts may be used. It is useful for classes, meetings, conferences, as well as theater audiences. Various scenes may be presented alone as experiences and discussion starters. Many colleges and religious, women's and aging organizations have used the play.

Scenes which can stand alone are scenes two and three in act one and scene one in act two. Some groups have presented, with good success, the whole of act one and other groups have presented with good success a combination of scene one and scene two from act one or a combination of scene two and three from act one.

For older women themselves or senior citizen service providers, some groups have used from page 35 where Mary asks, "Who am I?" through to the end of scene three. This part of scene three also appears in Ruth Jacobs' manual for group leaders, Older Women Surviving and Thriving, available for $18.95 plus $3 mailing from Family Service America, 11700 W. Lake Park Drive, Milwaukee, Wisconsin 53224.

There are no royalties required for presenting this play if no admission is charged by a non-profit organization. However, if admission is charged, even by a non-profit, royalties should be arranged with the author, Ruth Jacobs, 75 High Ledge Avenue, Wellesley, Massachusetts 02181, phone 617-237-1793. She is also available to lead discussion of the play or speak on women's issues and aging issues. She is a gerontologist, sociologist and poet.

At the end of the play, please see author's note on discussion.

Acknowledgements

All poems in the play are by the author. She would like to thank three artists' colonies for providing retreats so that she might work on the poetry and the play itself: The Edna St. Vincent Millay Colony, Ossabaw Island Foundation and Alfred University Summer Place. The author thanks the following individuals for suggestions and encouragement: Edith Jane Jacobs, daughter of the author, Ruth M. Murphy, M.D., Claire R. Cohen, Laura Lein, Peggy McIntosh, Carol Burdick, Pia Raffaele, Ellie Mamber, Julia and Gobin Stair, Elizabeth and David Dodson Gray and Rosalyn Feldberg. She also wishes to thank the Wellesley College Center for Research on Women, which premiered the mother/daughter segment. She thanks Elizabeth Freeman for believing in the play and publishing the original edition as a Crones Own Press book. She thanks Sandra Brown and Rita McCullough for reprinting as the author's third Knowledge, Ideas & Trends, Inc. (KIT) published book. KIT is indeed a positive publisher and a publisher the author respects and loves.

Cast In Order of Appearance

(Note: Whenever possible, the cast should be women of color as well as white women and women of all ethnic groups possible. However, the mother and daughter (Lisa and Ellen) and the Thin Woman and Fat Woman should be paired for similar characteristics. Actresses may play more than one part.)

RUTH, representing the author, a woman about 70.

MARMITA, an old woman.

JANE, a woman about 30.

THE CHORUS, made up of women of all types and ages, or one woman representing a chorus of women's voices.

ELLEN, a woman about 40.

LISA, a woman about 20.

JENNIFER, a woman about 30 (she should not be blond).

MARY, a woman about 50.

VIRGINIA, a woman about 60.

ELIZABETH, a woman about 70.

DORA, a woman about 80.

ALICE, a woman past ninety.

THIN WOMAN, middle aged.

FAT WOMAN, middle aged.

HELENE, a woman about 50.

PSYCHIATRIST, mid-life woman.

CATHERINE, a woman about 50.

SARA, a woman about 35.

CONSUELO, a woman about 45 (Latina).

LOIS, a woman about 70.

BETH, a woman about 25.

SISTER MARY CARITA, (Wears cross and short habit or simple dress.) Any age.

Act One

SCENE I   Who Speaks For Women?...3
SETTING: The Theater
CAST: Ruth, Marmita, Jane

SCENE II   In Between: In the Middle...13
SETTING: A kitchen
CAST: Chorus, Ellen, Lisa (The Chorus may
be a group of diverse women or one woman
speaking for all women.)

SCENE III Women Resting Together on Their
Ambivalences ...31
SETTING: Any living room
CAST: Lisa, Ellen, Jennifer, Mary, Virginia,
Elizabeth, Dora, Alice

Intermission, if desired

Act Two

SCENE I   Women Who Can't Rest on Their Ambivalences –
Four Vignettes...71
SETTINGS: A home, a bar, a psychiatrist's
office, and a jail cell.
CAST: Thin Self, Fat Self, Mary, Helene,
Psychiatrist, Catherine, Consuelo, Sara,
Lois, Beth, Sister Mary Caritas

SCENE II   Questioning and Celebrating...99
SETTING: The theater.
CAST: The entire cast as listed above.

AUTHOR'S NOTES...107

Act One

Act One

Who Speaks For Women?

Wearing a simple outfit with a long, tangled chain of buttons around her neck, Ruth walks onto the stage slowly, looks around at the audience and says:

> I am full of the voices of women.
> For nearly seventy years
> I have traveled this country
> and my life
> many lives listening.
> I must tell the stories of women
> who cannot speak for themselves
> who have been silenced
> or have spoken
> and not been heard.

Their voices exult, cry, plead, laugh, sigh, sing, assent and assert. Though the women's voices have individual tones and tunes, their words and themes are indeed a chorus. My drama is this chorus. But first you need to know about this woman before you who dares and cares to speak for women. We can only offer what we are. Everything we see or say is filtered through our own lives.

I parted my hair on the left side
the hair I had worn on the right
but the roots in stubborn treason
had directed it back by the night.

I am Ruth Harriet, granddaughter of Harriet who died before I was born, and granddaughter of Marmita and daughter of Jane. We all go back to our foremothers, though we often deny this. Let me tell about Marmita, born in Kiev, Ukraine. She came to Ellis Island where European immigrants to the United States were processed early in this century by officials who couldn't cope with foreign names.

My grandmother, Marmita
was given the name Minnie
at Ellis Island
and carefully traced it
on the report cards
of five children.
It was all the English
she could ever write.

When her oldest child,
my mother, died at thirty
she took a ten year old
and a three year old
and traced Minnie
on our report cards
and on all those forms
to get legal guardianship
and state aid to feed us.

She crocheted scarves
for the social workers

begged clothes and camps
and within a slum
kept a shining house.

Half-crazed
by her daughter's death
and endless poverty
she cried, screamed,
had no patience
with my brother
and even threatened me
too good though I was.

But every spring
somewhere in that slum
she stole lilacs
to put upon my bureau
and trace her love
forever on me.

It is only recently that I wrote that poem. I have just begun to understand my grandmother as I have myself aged. I empathize as I see what it is to be a woman whose options are limited by age, gender, roles and fate.

One morning last year I searched my Grandmother's button jar to match a button. Grandma gave me the jar shortly before her death at age 87, decades ago. As I sifted through the buttons, I realized how old some were. I also had visions of her life. There were buttons cut from the clothes she had sewed from necessity for her five children and from friends' hand-me-downs she altered for my brother and me. I remembered she had sewed late at night, exhausted after her day's chores. Yet women like her had been unvalued and not counted as part of the labor force because they had worked at home.

In the jar were military buttons cut from the uniforms of her sons with tears and relief after the wars. There were several glittering buttons saved from the few good dresses she had owned, bought for her children's high school graduations and weddings.

Suddenly, I, certainly no craftsperson, needed desperately to make something from my grandmother's buttons. Though my college students' papers waited, I began in a compulsive, even frenzied way to string the buttons on strong thread. Without forethought, I strung the buttons in a random way and then tangled them together as Grandma's life was strung and tangled not by her design or desire but by the needs of others.

(Marmita enters.)

MARMITA: Yes, I really never had much choice. In Ukraine, I loved a young man, but my parents instead made me marry your Grandfather. I never really loved Avrom. But I did my duty. When he was jailed for opposing the Czar, I bribed the guard and went to the jail wearing two sets of clothes and smuggled my husband out in women's clothes.

Then I left everybody I cared about to escape by steerage with him to America. After all, he was the father of my child, your mother.

I was only twenty but had already had three infants and your mother was the only one who lived. My first daughter died shortly after birth, as did your mother's boy twin. It was my second pregnancy in two years. I was worn out and did not have enough milk to feed both twins. In those days there was only breast feeding. Your mother was the frailer twin so I gave the boy to a strong peasant woman to nurse. It was a hard choice. She fed her own baby first and there was not enough for my boy.

You know, all my life I saved everything but I couldn't save my own children. Five of my seven children, those two babies, and your mother and another daughter and a son died before me. And it was so hard to bring them up. Your grandfather never made a good living. I shopped so frugally. I sewed and took in boarders. During Prohibition, I made and sold wine. But it wasn't that dangerous. The police were my best customers and they protected me.

When my son enlisted in the Marines below the legal age and was sent to fight in Nicaragua, I went to the Mayor and got him out. But I couldn't save your mother when she got cancer and died. I used to go to the park and cry so she would not see me. When we were together, I pretended I didn't know she was dying and she pretended she didn't know. She must have cried alone too.

RUTH:
It would have been better for you both if you had not hidden it and had cried together.

MARMITA:
Maybe, but in those days it was different and we kept our feelings secret. But it got harder and harder not to cry openly when your Uncle George and your Aunt Ida died. It made me crazy angry and I blamed their mates, everybody, the world. When your father collapsed, it was hard to take care of you and your brother, but I think being needed kept me going.

I always wanted to be needed. When I was old and even poorer, I used to walk around the city streets looking for handkerchiefs men had dropped. I would wash them and iron the handkerchiefs and give them to you for your husband so I would have something to give you.

RUTH:
You gave me courage. You taught me how to go on when my firstborn died as a toddler. And when you insisted on being in the old age home because you didn't want to burden anyone, you begged me to bring you my family's clothes to mend and I did even if I had to pull off buttons or rip the clothes first. You made me so many afghans that I had no places to put them. And you worried when I got three university degrees between 35 and 45 that I was neglecting my children. You didn't see a need for higher education for women, especially

married ones. How were you to know that my marriage would end in divorce after thirty years?

(Marmita leaves. Jane comes on stage.)

JANE: When I was dying those two years and you and your brother were so small, I was insane with pain and worry about what would happen to you two. When you didn't take care of your brother or clean the house, I said to you, "You will be sorry when I am dead." And then I felt guilty. Did I make you feel guilty?

RUTH: Yes. It took me years and much help to get over that. I am still not over it completely. But you couldn't help it. You also loved me and I you and I named my daughter after you.

> I, once briefly a daughter
> now always a daughter
> dream of daughter.
> She is the mirror
> in which I see
> my mother's eyes
> look back at me.

I was only ten when you died, but you had given me enough by then to make a life on. And other women gave me what you could not.

> From my mother
> the love of poems

and violets.
From my grandmother
giving when
there was little
left to give.
From one aunt
an artist's eye
and from another,
courage despite
recurrent tragedy.
From a near-mother,
competence at work
and from still
another nurturer
keeping compassion
within the bounds
of self-respect.

JANE: Did my friends help you?

RUTH: Oh, I forgot that. Yes, the dentist's wife made her husband fill Larry's teeth and mine free. Another made her husband give me my first job. A third bought me a winter coat.

The motherless
have many
mothers.

It wasn't surprising. Through life, women often help others. I experienced this after my divorce when   I   moved   into   an   Italian-American neighborhood full of nurturers.

Across the yards
abundant with tomatoes
zucchini, eggplant, peppers
and the blessed grape,
my neighbors' Italian voices
comfort me with liquid sounds.

Domenic, Adelina,
Joseph, Yolanda
call me Ruthie
wondering at this Jew,
this strange professor,
who types into the night.

Even as I write this,
the phone rings.
It is Adelina, eighty-two
who senses I think of her
and tells me not to cook.
She is bringing pasta
for my dinner
her perfect poem.

She made me, a stranger,
welcome here.
Like her garden,
I flourish with her love.

(Jane leaves.)

RUTH: As a child, I envied girls whose mothers took
care of them. It was a mystery to me why so
many hated their mothers. When I grew up, I

wondered why adult women often disliked and avoided older women. Now, I understand. Women's lives in this society are often painful and young women see in their mothers their own future dilemmas.

Act One

SCENE II

In Between: In the Middle

(The chorus recites. One woman can represent the chorus.)

I am a woman
in between
in the middle
pulled by others' tides
and even by my own.

In between waking and sleeping
in between sleeping and waking
halfway from birth to death
childhood and old age
I glimpse my strengths
and weaknesses
courage and fears
desires and limitations
joys and sorrows
hope and despair
fear and faith.

I am between
wanting marriage
and wanting singleness
wanting children
and wanting my time.
I am in the middle of
lovers and former lovers
siblings
parents and my children
my husband and my children
and his children
his parents and mine
the empty nest and the refilled
children and their spouses
children and their children
job and home
work and pleasure
work and more work
supervisor and supervisees
my husband's retirement and
my renaissance
friends and foes
friends and other friends
adulthood and studenthood
the generations before
and those ahead
home and the world.

I am torn between
ambition for my daughter
and knowledge of
the risks and costs
the rewards and

cruelties awaiting
as women assert
and are punished.

I am between
anxiety and confidence
activity and passivity
assertion and diffidence
trust and mistrust
hope and hopelessness
dreams and nightmares
love and hate
menstruation and menopause
triumph and defeat
growth and stagnation
nurturing and resenting
hurting and healing
self interest and selflessness
sensuality and celibacy
spirituality and intellectuality
dependence and independence
my thin and fat selves
relaxation and stress
humor and pathos
myself and others
and parts of myself.

I am in the middle of
war and peace
radicalism and conservatism
private concerns and political action
activism and retreatism
feminism and backlash

convenience and the environment
my country and universality.

I am a woman
in between
in the middle
pulled by others' tides
and even by my own.

I am a woman
in the middle
in between
wanting to help
and wanting help
happy
discontented
free
fettered
fearless
frightened
frank.

I am a woman
in between
who I was
and who
I shall yet be
I am Me
groaning
groping
growing
skimming the waters
testing the waters

swimming against the tides
sinking
surfacing
splashing
getting wet
and wetting others.

I am in the middle
of a new ocean
but will not drown;
my ambivalences
will be islands
to rest upon
with other women
between our thrusts
toward a shore
as yet uncharted
and even denied.

I am a woman
in between
in the middle
pulled by others' tides
and by my own.

(Enter Ellen, a mother, and Lisa, her daughter.)

ELLEN: The poem applies to me.
                     It is hard to be a mother

                          Who will feed the feeder
                          Who will nurture the nurturers
                          Who will help the helpers

Who will counsel the counselors
and when?

LISA: The poem applies to me.

It is hard to be a daughter
My mother is a mirror
of what I do not wish to be
I want no ambivalences

What of darkness fear I
if I know no fear?
What of weakness hear I
if I will not hear?
What of pain or sorrow
if I close my eyes
need I fear tomorrow?

ELLEN: Dream on little wise one
deny any weakling senses
waking life, my darling
silences defenses

LISA: What a pain you are.

You remind me of those homeless pitiful bag
ladies wandering around the streets carrying
their rags in bags.

ELLEN: We are all bag ladies
or becoming so.
Nothing lasts
not love

or the beloved
or hope
even mountains crumble
only the ocean waits
to catch our tears

Bags of memories
tell us who we were
before we were wise
The bags burden us.
Carrying about
our losses,
we stumble
clutching our unfreedom
against all threats
or promises
it being all we have
it being all we know
it being all we are.

LISA: You sure feel sorry for yourself. You make me
feel guilty for growing up. You make me want
to get away from you even more.

You should try harder
You sound like a martyr.
I suggest that you
turn anger into art
a crust of bread
into bread pudding
old chickens are tough
they survived the axe

even bag ladies manage
why not you?

ELLEN: I do not like what I am.

I have tried to find new roles.
Men my age prefer you.
Employers prefer you too.
They seem to say:

You can't trust older women
they put philodendron
on the file cabinets
dump real coffee grinds
into wastebaskets
and even hang posters
in the washrooms.

Next thing you know
they will be asking
for a raise because
they made the place
feel like someplace
you might like to be
if they weren't there
looking down their noses
when you cheat or lie
to the customers.

LISA: I think you exaggerate this age discrimination bit. Older women aren't the only ones who have problems. Young women have troubles too.

ELLEN: I know.

                Before we are accustomed
                to our bodies and our minds
                they are after them.
                We nurture before we are
                comfortable in our skins.

                Then, when we know
                the joys of flesh
                and wisdom shared
                we are eager to meet
                a world that has
                lost interest.

LISA: I sure know what you mean. Guys are after us
                all the time. Being young and pretty isn't
                always a bargain. You have to fend them off. It
                must be hard though when they aren't there to
                fend off.

                I worry sometimes.
                Will this long hair
                turn gray and dry?
                Will my Prince Charming
                turn into a frog?
                Should I even worry about such trivia?
                I went to Washington
                and to New York to demonstrate
                but they didn't really hear.
                Will there be a world left
                for me to grow old in?

Should I have children
will they be able to grow up?

ELLEN: Are you really that discouraged?

LISA: It is not like the seventies, Mom.

The gentle bearded young men
have gone into the corporate offices
or are driving taxis
toward the graveyard
of their dreams for social change.

The long haired women in ragged jeans
have cut their hair and hopes
and joined the secretarial
or data processing pool.

The libraries are being boarded up
the teachers sent from the schools
public transport is in trouble
public welfare is dead
and social justice also.
ONLY MUNITIONS PROSPER.

ELLEN: And I thought you and your friends had it all. I
                think it was simpler for my mother, your
                grandmother. God knows she worked hard
                doing for others and suffered sexism but she
                thought things would be better for me and
                for you... Her generation believed in progress.
                Mine is discouraged. Yours believes in doom.

LISA: Oh, it's not that bad. Sometimes I worry about the world but mostly I am concerned with me. I guess I really think the world will go on. In fact, the major problem I feel is fear of failure, not measuring up and in some way failing my standards. I feel pressure to do something special, something definite and concrete with my life. Grandma didn't think she had to do it all and maybe you didn't either and maybe that was easier.

ELLEN: Well, I used to think I shouldn't expect too much out of life but being a good wife and mother and friend and being good to others generally. Listen to how that feels now.

> Sometimes when
> exhausted by hard work
> and work for others
> I refuse to rest
> reminding myself
> that people
> in concentration camps
> dropped in exhaustion
> that refugees or POWs
> walked or rowed
> to death.
>
> I identify
> with the wretched
> making myself wretched
> punishing myself
> for imagined guilts

driving myself
serving others
worrying about them

Perhaps I am
an exaggeration case
but we share
this woman syndrome.
We were taught it
and not just
by our mothers.

I deserve better
daughter, you deserve better.
I deserve, you deserve
to rest when tired
to eat when hungry
good carefully chosen food
nourishing instead of cheap
or leftover.

I deserve, you deserve
self love
and being loved
I deserve my choices
and first choice.
I deserve a decent
humane society.
I deserve success
and rewards
I deserve to trust myself
as others trust me.

I deserve to forgive myself
as I forgive others.

I deserve
not to be stepped upon
and to cry out
when I hurt.
I deserve to have righteous
indignation
and to stop making excuses
for others
and start making them
for myself.

I deserve
to allow myself
the seemingly trivial
I deserve new clothes
not always clothes on sale
I deserve fresh sheets
and fragrant flowers.

I deserve
you deserve
not to have to do
ABSOLUTELY EVERYTHING
AND FOR EVERYONE.

Although I will continue
concern for the wretched
I have a right to happiness.
I must take care of myself

as I continue to give
to others including you, daughter.

If I can only nurture others
if I cannot nurture myself
if I am tired all the time
what do I teach my daughter
what do we teach all our daughters
and our sons?

How much social change
is needed.
How much unlearning
we must do
to claim the joy
that is our right
our need
our survival!

LISA: I understand. I am glad you feel we deserve. I
am sorry I am so hard on you. You've seen I
am really scared though I've been afraid to
show it. And I need to push you away so I can
be free.

If only I could look at us
here, now and today, standing
as independent travelers
who shared a trip
now pasted neatly in an album
of casual reminiscence.

If only I no longer waited
to reenact that journey
exposed and small
as I was once
bringing you my infant hurts
and blaming you for them.

If only we could snap the cord
that pulls a raw red furrow
deep across your open heart and mine.
If only we could break that hateful rope
and yet not make of it a noose
to hang that tenderness
which once was what I grew upon,
then you and I might compromise
end this present bitter journey
embark upon some new and separate ones
keeping our luggage light and apart
greeting each other as we pass
and welcoming our new companies freely.

ELLEN: I know you must take your own journey to a place where I cannot go or choose even though I try to give you maps you refuse. Find that place and enjoy the finding. Sometimes I mourn my child gone and try to keep you as one. Please grow and go with as little pain as possible for both of us and with my love and pride.

LISA: Though now we stand against the door
                reliving history once more,
                I shall be free as you would have me free

and armed enough to bear the pain of parting
and leaving you, go on with hope to see
this present tense of life now starting.

Please know your gifts of life and love
are maps I take along
but I must feel by day and night
that I am I for once
and I am strong.

Mom, what will you do now?

ELLEN: I am not sure.

I am a woman
in between
in the middle
pulled by others' tides
and even by my own.

I am in the middle
of a new ocean
but will not drown
my ambivalences
will be islands
to rest upon
with other women
including you, daughter
between our thrusts
toward a shore
as yet uncharted
and even denied
BUT THERE IS A SHORE.

LISA:

I am a woman
in between
who I was
and who
I shall yet be
I am me
groaning
groping
growing
skimming the waters
testing the waters
swimming against the tides
sinking
surfacing
splashing
getting wet
and wetting others
including you, mother *(she laughs)*
AND I WILL NOT DROWN.

ELLEN and LISA:

WE are women
in between
in the middle
of a troubled world
pulled by others' tides
and even by our own.

(Ellen and Lisa embrace. They remain on the stage.)

Act One

SCENE III

Women Resting On Their Ambivalences

(Lisa and Ellen remain on the stage and are joined by six other women. One is about thirty, one about fifty, one about sixty, one about seventy, one about eighty, and one past ninety. The women carry large, round brightly colored pillows and two of them carry extra pillows which they hand to Ellen and Lisa. The eight women seat themselves on the cushions in a semi-circle in the following order: Lisa, then Jennifer, the thirty year old, Ellen, then Mary, the fifty year old, then Virginia, the sixty year old, then Elizabeth, the seventy year old, then Dora, the eighty year old, then Alice, past ninety. Chairs may be used instead of pillows.)

LISA: Sitting here feels like school. Remember when we sat and played button, button, who has the button? Well, you just heard my story. Jennifer, you are the next oldest. You take the button.

(Lisa hands a large button to Jennifer.)

JENNIFER: So it is my turn.

Who am I?
I am what I do.
THEY pay me to be
SOMEBODY and that is
why my WORK is really me
and if you don't believe that
you haven't been brought up right.
You must be a foreigner or one of those
people left over from the early seventies
who thought we were going to find ourselves
someplace besides the office or on the couches.

LISA: Is that how you function?

JENNIFER: Functionaires
                         can only function
                         at functions.

                         Empty rooms
                         empty them
                         of roles.

                         Terrified,
                         they function
                         to create functions.

                         Functions thus
                         are functional
                         when empty.

                         Functionaries
                         are empty
                         through functioning.

Functionaires
deserve pity
for terror.

Who today
is not
a functionary?

Functioning
is after all
functional.

ELLEN: It sounds pretty grim.

JENNIFER: I get by.

Put work beside your bed
make lists
contract your services
do the extras
fill every hour
tell people
you are always busy
and be that way.

If you fall
asleep in the sun
drink coffee
and run.

ALICE: I guess it has worked for you. You are a success.

JENNIFER: Yes, I suppose so, but:

The world's over ripe plums
splatter into weary hands
which hurl them on the ground
like bloody, useless things.
These are not the fruits desired
It is not enough to be admired.

Forget I said that. This is an off day for me and
this group is where I let down. I really am lucky
to have a decent job these days. I tell myself,
"So what if there is no Mr. Right?"

You had better settle for work
love is for the young
the blond
the lithe
the lucky
the others.

You are a workhorse
pulling weights
piling weights
putting weights
upon yourself.

Learn to love your work
or talk a good line.
Maybe someone will
pat you
pet you
"nice horsey."

ELLEN: You're not missing that much if you don't marry. I read somewhere that single women are the happiest, healthiest women in America. Marriage is better for men than women.

JENNIFER: Yes, Ellen, but the grass is always greener elsewhere... You already talked so if you don't mind I'll give the button to Mary.

ELLEN: Okay.

(Jennifer gets up, passes the button to Mary and returns to her seat.)

MARY: Who am I?

I was a wife for thirty years. One day my husband decided he didn't want to be married anymore to an older woman, though he was, of course, four years older than I. I've always thought it had something to do with the fact that his company passed him over for a promotion. He was stuck in a dead end job he hated while younger fellows were zooming past him. Anyway, he had affairs with women much younger than himself. Thank God our children were grown and out of the house. Finally, he made one woman half his age pregnant and he married her after our divorce. Now they have two babies and I suppose he feels important at home, if not at work.

As for me, I remember going shopping shortly after he left. I kept walking around the market

without putting anything in my cart. Suddenly,
I realized I didn't even know what I liked to
eat. For years, I had been buying what he
liked and what the children liked and that's
what I ate. I didn't even know my own taste in
food. How was I going to make a life for
myself? Though I was pretty depressed that
Sunday I went to a singles' brunch I saw
advertised in the newspaper. I got all dressed
up. I guess I hoped to find a man.

Well, the woman who ran the club came up to
me and said, "Please don't come back, you're
too old for this group." I looked around. The
men were my age or lots older. I was
devastated. Of course, I had gray hair then.
(She laughs) I have colored it since.

LISA: What did you do besides color your hair?

MARY: I cried a lot. At first it was utter despair.

Leaving the suburb and wifehood
for a cheaper city apartment
I moved my plants in first
so something would greet me.

The first morning I awoke
at dawn to see the rats' ballet
a strange and frenzied circle
beneath my window and said
"there are worse things than rats."

Strange things were happening to me.

In what is one to believe?
The city screams at you
and you scream back,
finding your voice
someone else's shrill cry.

JENNIFER: I guess you were scared.

MARY: Yes and more than that.

I envied those women
whose husbands tucked them
into cars and beds
and paid their dinner checks.
My so-called freedom
felt like unconnectedness.
I thought, some day
I will stay in bed forever
and no one will care
or even know.

I hated married women and was foolish enough
to think they were all happy. Once, I even wrote
an imaginary letter to a suburbanite.

You,
with your small mouth
and long tennis legs,
living with antiques
a husband and roses,
don't know what it is

to live alone on women's
tiny wages that buy
starches and roaches.
Uncordially
yours.

LISA: You had a right to be angry, I think.

MARY: Yes, and I wanted revenge.

Before I saw my former husband again:

I wanted to be loved
or at least desired
and possessed
so that the creeping mildew
of soul and body
would not be intensified
by the sight and smell of him
my lost and only lover
of a long and wasted life
destroyed by his rejection.

I covered up my pain with bravado, I thought:

Not wanting to turn to salt,
I won't look back.
Salt is tears
tears are acid rain
and acid rain corrodes.

I told myself:

There are other fish in the sea
and I will fry them.
There are other rocks on the shore
and I will throw them.
There are other men in the world
and I will try them.

But it didn't work. There were a few nibbles
but I didn't land any fish.

I didn't know how lonely I was
until I met him.
I said, "I am divorced."
He said, "His loss is
some other man's gain."
I answered, too honestly,
"there is no other man"
and hoped there might be.
He was silent then
and forever, after.

ELLEN: Yes. Men are often afraid of getting involved. I
              know how you felt to be rejected.

MARY: Do you?

              Humiliating
              to wait
              at fifty
              for a call
              for a word
              for a kiss

from a man
hardly known,
pushing aside
proven women,
fine friends,
to chase
his scent,
knowing
it is better
to wait
for a call
never coming
than not
to wait
or want
at all.

LISA: Do you still feel that way?

MARY: No, at least not often. I accept my singleness. It
               happened rather suddenly.

Once, passing a certain place
I joyously contemplated
being there
then realized
it was the sort of place
my husband and I
had often been
together.

For the very first time
I really knew

what all those legalities
had failed
to teach.

My marriage was as dead
as my youth
and all my mourning
and seeking
would not bring
them back.

Since then I have gained strength. Joining this support group has helped. It was good I did because I had a set-back when my boss fired me to hire a young, pretty secretary.

We will
work hard
for low wages
gratefully BUT
THEY much prefer
our daughters and
even granddaughters.

The unwanted cringe
our backs ache
our eyes dull
we even stop
thinking we
are worth
HIRING.

JENNIFER: I remember. You were pretty depressed then. We had to help restore your self confidence. We nagged you to get some training for a better job.

MARY: It wasn't easy but I did take the courses. And you all encouraged me through them and through the awful job search. You, Jennifer, gave me a good lead that led to a new job. It's lucky I changed jobs because at my new place there are other women alone. Doing things with them helps me cope with the Noah's Ark Syndrome.

          They are still coming
          two by two off the ark.

          Hostesses do not invite
          unescorted single women
          divorcees or even widows
          expecting they will rape
          husbands, steal homes, or
          worst trauma of all, mean
          an odd number at table.

          What kind of orgies
          need such pairings?

ELIZABETH: You make me feel terrible. It's true I haven't often included my widowed women friends when my husband and I invite our coupled friends over. But I really thought the singles would be uncomfortable. It isn't that I didn't want them. As a matter of fact, sometimes I do ask one, she refuses to come because she would be the only single. It's a two way street.

Well, I'm sorry I interrupted you but I had to say that.

I was wondering, did you finally get used to the city?

MARY: It WAS hard that first winter. I didn't think I would make it. But I did.

        I rushed to the ocean
        during the February thaw
        to find dried sea grass
        waving tall and golden
        undefeated by the storms.
        There by the shore
        I danced with the grass
        exulting at my strength
        to bear aloneness,
        shouting to the grass
        "we have weathered
        the winter
        you and I
        we are kin
        we are kin
        we are kin."

I felt proud of coping.

I have learned
to blow the horn
threaten landlords,
utility companies,
and meter maids,
use public parks,
thrift shops,
and free clinics,
insult insulters,
ignore accosters,
trust strangers,
when feasible
see rainbows
in the gutters
find in alleys
parking spaces
boxes for bookcases
wild flowers
even furniture.

Now I sleep through
neighbors' parties,
drown out trucks
with Beethoven,
fix doorknobs,
outwit pay toilets,
swim at hotels
though not registered.

A new city kid
at fifty
learns fast.

Well, I am very sorry I took so long to tell my story. Virginia, here's the button.

(Mary passes the button to Virginia.)

VIRGINIA: I'm glad things are better now, Mary. I used to think being divorced was easier than being widowed. When someone dies you blame yourself. You say, "what did I do wrong?" You feel guilty for living.

MARY: Women blame themselves for divorce too. They ask, "what did I do wrong to make him behave that way?" They even blame themselves when their children get divorced. Since we have so little power in the world, we over exaggerate our importance in the family which is the only place many of us are allowed to feel important.

VIRGINIA: I guess so. Anyway, I know a lot of women lose husbands through divorce or death. There are lots of widows around because men marry younger women and die younger. But it seemed at first as if I was the only one. I understand, Mary, about your letter to a suburbanite. We were best friends with our neighbors and after Ralph's death it seemed:

> Wherever I went
> they were always together
> She was the echo
> of his steps
> and he drew in her closeness

like a fragrance.
Silent and close,
they dreamt by the fire
spent as the embers.
simple with loving.
Watching their unison,
I yearned
for moments
that never again
would be
for me, for me, for me.

Oh, I did my share of crying too. I suppose it is
good I did.

If I had to give advice to others I'd say:

When a loved one is dying
go into the woods and cry.
Only pure beauty
like the sight of sun on water
or birdsongs in loved trees
that he will never share again
will bring those tears
for his darkness and yours.

The clumsy comfort of friends
and the strange running
or bargaining you will do,
will only make a tighter vise
about your throbbing head
and angry throat.

Go alone to beauty.
Mourn your aloneness and weep
for the loved one
and for yourself
and for the fragility of life
when the world shared
is so beautiful.

In the end we are all alone
but there is still beauty;
it is eternal
and so are memories
alive in us.

For me the memory of Ralph is very strong. I
am not a single at heart. I can't go to bars or
clubs like some women alone do seeking to end
singleness, at least for one night.

I know times have changed but I haven't.

I suppose I am still his.
Sometimes I have thought
the pressure of another body
would wipe away his imprint
but my desire flows backward
stubborn as the tide
to the wedding bed
so I wear his ring still,
cursing the throat lump
that certain music brings.

ALICE: Weren't you ever angry at what happened to you?

VIRGINIA: Certainly.

              Once I baked bread
              and because I had
              to eat it alone,
              threw half
              into the yard
              for the dogs.

              I even went through a period of isolation and self pity. I shut myself away, thinking;

              Plants are more predictable
              than people.
              If you give plants
              enough water
              light and warmth
              they will reward you.

              People, on the other hand,
              even given
              considerable attention,
              may forget you
              or become hostile
              or even die
              Begonias are better.

              I was actually mad at my children and grandchildren for being occupied with their own lives. I hated the empty nest. I felt:

I had no home
there was no love in those walls
which enclosed my grief
no comfort in plants and colors
with which I tried to deceive.

There cannot be a home for one
where there had been many.
A woman alone becomes an orphan
crying in the night
with only cold walls to hear.

ELLEN: You seem alright now. It is hard to believe you were like that. How did you get to feeling better?

VIRGINIA: I'm not sure. Maybe time. Maybe my need and strength to survive.

One day I was ready
to give up
what seemed
an impossible life.

The next day
there was light
and air
and energy.
The dark had gone
as quickly as it came.

I could exult
again at music

and at the sight
of sun on snow.

The papers
I had thrown about
to signal my despair
could be put in neat
and manageable piles.

I could do
what needed
to be done
and what before
seemed a task
beyond endurance.

Even though I had lost him
I would not wear black
and put on Spring colors
being as I was meant to be.

Yesterday I mourned.
Today I have life to celebrate
I have myself.

I realized it was not my fault Ralph was dead
and that he would want me to enjoy life. I
began to do things and take as many trips as I
could afford. If not now, when? I am luckier
financially than many widows.

At the slightest invitation
I bed down in strange cities.

From my lair in Bedford Square
I took London in a week.
Paris is in my harem now
and Aberdeen and Amsterdam
and Bath and Berkeley too.

New York and Washington are mine
I have dallied with Chicago,
San Francisco and Tucson,
Puerto de la Cruz and Marrakesh
I do not love you less
because I made Atlanta mine.

If I cannot have lovers
I shall have cities.
Sixty cannot be coy
as twenty with lovers
waiting in the wings.
I go boldly to conquer cities
Who is to judge of consummations
and compensations?

I also decided when home to get out daily for
exercise and seeing people. I joined the "Y" and
began to use the pool.

We are sweatless
and weightless
purity personified,
our rhythmic motion
comforting as we
unite with fluids

of our individual
and species birth.

We are grateful
for oceans
lakes and pools
where body merges
intimately with
perfect medium
so even those
unlucky or clumsy
everywhere else
glide and hide
gracefully into
crystal refuge.

ELLEN: Swimming works off sexual energy too.

VIRGINIA: Yes, I know. If they knew how sensuous swimming was, they might ban it. I am in the exercise class at the "Y" too. Also, I made some terrific new women friends there including Elizabeth whom I brought tonight to this group. Elizabeth is a dedicated, almost full time volunteer at the "Y" and other places. She got me into volunteering and that helped me too. The least I could do was get her into this group. And, now the least I can do is give Elizabeth her turn to talk.

(She hands Elizabeth the button.)

ELIZABETH: Well, I've been listening to all your troubles and feel lucky that at seventy I still have my husband. He is special -- a truly faithful and kind man. Not all men are like your ex, Mary. Our marriage has lasted fifty years. So far we have our health, are enjoying life and can help others. It feels good to be seventy.

> Seventy is being outside
> on a November day
> knowing the fragility
> of sunshine.
>
> Seventy is facing lost causes
> and fighting on
> having little to lose.
>
> Seventy is loss
> and dry tears unseen
> but also passion
> and private jokes
> suddenly revealed by life.
>
> Seventy is waking early
> to seek treasures
> which there is no room
> to hold.
>
> Seventy is sensing
> which stranger
> will give the ecstasy
> of friendship
> and who will betray.

At seventy
you grasp wisdom
in your hands
while they
are still strong.

Go into seventy
hoping and loving
you will be women
made beautiful
by having lived
well and long.

VIRGINIA: You give me courage to get older.

ELIZABETH: Thanks. I've decided what is important in life. We tend to obsess sometimes about nothings. I'm beyond that now.

Having climbed the mountain,
I came down the other side
carrying carefully mementoes
collected with great effort
going up.

Halfway down I stopped
and suddenly hurled away
those no longer treasures
amazed I had cherished
such burdens.

I have learned to live for each day and be grateful for it. We women are lucky because we

love to nurture and can nurture through life,
though not always in the same way we did once.
I love being a senior volunteer and 1 love days
like the one I had at the beach last May.

I lust for the ocean.
In May when sunners huddle
with shawls on the beach,
I swim the waves alone
warm with joy.

My sole ownership was challenged
when Amy, seven and a half,
introduced herself
and asked how to float.

"Don't be afraid
and you won't sink," I said.
She replied. "I'll play dead."
"Not dead," I told her,
"Just relax -- the water holds."

Neither of us cold
seventy swam with seven.
I taught her how to float
while her parents sunned
and Amy stroked my toes
in gratitude, teaching love.

Wherever you go, Amy
I shall go.
In the Spring you are seventy,
you will recall

how a May swimmer
taught you courage.

Though I shall be long gone
I will live then in you
my child and my sister.

Yes, life is good. The only thing I worry about is that my health may fail or that Jim will get sick, or that I will become senile.

Even my children grow old
I see my years
written on their once soft faces
now wise and worn.

I hope at eighty I can still do the things I love.
Dora, what is it like to be eighty?

(She hands the button to Dora.)

DORA: You are the same as you have always been, a little achey sometimes and slower and forgetful. Yet within you are all the things you ever were and more.

Two years past eighty
I forget a lot of things
I don't want to remember
like watching my words.
I remember a lot of things
I thought I had forgotten
like Miss Brown

who made kindergarten
another home.

Two years past eighty
I own my old body
with all its imperfections
and like myself.

Two years past eighty
I spot a new bird
learn a wildflower's name
see a great grandchild smile
hear live, for the first time
Bach's Sonata in C Major,
tell the President off,
drink a new wine,
and make new friends
of you.

There are a lot of good things. However, the bad
thing is some people don't see YOU at all. They
see only age and reject and belittle you because
of that. It makes me furious when they talk to
me as if I were a child. Mad turned inward
becomes sad so I express my anger. I say to the
world:

I am in this old body
but not of it.
My mind runs barefoot
unwinded along the ocean
and my spirit climbs
mountains.

> Who are you
> to judge me unfit
> and unlovable
> when I so love
> this world
> and human touch?

You know some people never touch old people as if they are repulsive. When I was in the hospital, I noticed that the interns and medical students stood practically across the room from me. And they couldn't wait to get out of the room. It was different for young patients. Old folks have the same needs as other people for closeness. I let them know how I felt about it. I'll make a prediction:

> I will leave as I came
> screaming pain.
> I shall not accept with grace
> the indignities of age
> and the indignities to age
> but exit -- not too soon --
> decrying my doom,
> hating my fate,
> protesting my loss,
> pushing back the end,
> with every angry breath.

ELIZABETH: I like what you said. I admire your guts. I need to learn how to be eighty in a world insensitive to older people. Can you be specific about how to handle folks when they treat us as stupid because we are old.

DORA: I'll give you an example.

                   The electric company
                   overcharges me
                   but there is nowhere else
                   I can buy electricity.
                   I call to complain
                   they say yes
                   but still overcharge.

                   I will keep calling
                   and talking.
                   How much an hour
                   do they pay
                   their telephone clerks?

ELIZABETH: Not bad. It gives me some ideas.

VIRGINIA: I know what Dora and Elizabeth mean about ageism. I feel it already at sixty and get angry too.

ALICE: When you turn ninety, they think you are an idiot.

MARY: Certainly at fifty you experience it, as I told you.

ELLEN: And at forty.

JENNIFER: Even at thirty, the double standard of aging exists. Men and employers bypass you for the twenty year olds.

LISA: At college, many senior men prefer the freshman girls.

DORA: Ageism is a common disease. You learn to live with it but you should try hard to do what you can about it. Don't wait until my age to fight ageism. Also, more young women have to prepare for aging by getting to know older women. I'm glad I have you all as friends. I lost my husband and many friends to death. A few of my friends older than I do not recognize me. But I have come to some reconciliation with my losses.

No love is lost
even though the lover
turns away from us
or life.

Within us are the people
we have loved,
not as they were
but as we wanted
them to be.

As our fresh grief
softens to sorrow,
we suddenly discover
the lover's eyes

in our mirror
the lover's words
on our lips,
even the beloved's jokes
have become ours.

What reality has taken,
we have taken
for our own.
Nothing is ever lost.
Layers of our being
contain all that has
lived for us
or that we imagined.

We exude
the strength
of our losses
and our gains glow
even in the dark.

All in all, friends, being eighty or ninety or one
hundred is not bad considering the alternative.
You should know that Alice.

ALICE: Nearer one hundred than ninety
                               I have some arthritis pains
                               but no pain about the past
                               and each morning is a gift.

I never married but loved my primary schoolers
for almost fifty years. Some of my students
and the younger teachers visit and send me

cards. Some look older than me. I guess I have good genes.

When I retired, I traveled on cheap tours everywhere. You should do things when you can so you won't be eaten by regrets later. I can't travel anymore but I close my eyes and see Florence, Paris and lots of places. I have good memories. I also do as much as I can now. There are great activities in the elderly housing complex where I live and I go to everything including the exercise class. We do the exercises while sitting in chairs.

I gave up my driver's license years ago but I walk everyday that weather permits. I use a cane to get around but I have decorated it with great decals – see. I use a magnifying glass to read the newspaper and I love the large print books and books on tape.

You know, there are a lot of women my age these days and even some men. Maybe I'll reach 100 and be greeted on television like all those centenarians.

But, like Dora, I am troubled by ageism. When my niece drives me to the doctor, he talks to her as if I am a child. He asks her the questions and gives her the information. That infuriates me. Also, the younger residents of my elderly housing complex, look down on us who live in the assisted living section. To get back at them, I put a basket of marbles on the shelf outside my apartment to show I haven't lost my marbles.

I hope I never have to go to the nursing unit, but if I do, I'll take my marbles with me. I volunteer now visiting the nursing home patients who have no visitors.

VIRGINIA: Good for you. We are also lucky you come to this group. We were afraid you'd drop out when you moved to the retirement building.

ALICE: I may live in an old age ghetto for safety and convenience but I want to be with people of all ages also. I thank you for taking turns driving me here. You are good friends. I hope one of you will give the eulogy at my funeral. I've pre-paid my funeral, you know.

ELLEN: We hope that won't be for a long time.

ALICE: Don't mourn me when I go, Ellen. I had a good long life and I am not afraid to die. Now that I am this old, I feel close to God and never feel lonely. I hope I will go quickly when my time comes and not suffer. I have signed a Living Will saying "no heroic measures."

Two things comfort me. I recite the Lord is my Shepherd psalm every day. Also, I remember that when I moved into assisted living, I gave my books to the library for others to enjoy. I also gave away to younger people practically all the mementoes I collected on my travels. It is good to know other people are enjoying them and will think of me when I go to that big primary school in the sky. *(She laughs.)*

JENNIFER: I love that painting from Mexico you gave me.

ALICE: I'm glad.

All in all, folks
I'm alive
I'm well
I survive
I survive well.

Well, to survive as well as I do, I need my rest. I think it is time to end this meeting. If anyone has anything else to say, you better do it fast.

Lisa stands and says:

I'm alive
I'm well
I survive
I survive well.

Jennifer stands and says:

I'm alive
I'm well
I survive
I survive well.

Ellen stands and says:

> I'm alive
> I'm well
> I survive
> I survive well.

Mary stands and says:

> I'm alive
> I'm well
> I survive
> I survive well.

Virginia stands and says:

> I'm alive
> I'm well
> I survive
> I survive well.

Elizabeth stands and says:

> I'm alive
> I'm well
> I survive
> I survive well.

Dora stands and says:

> I'm alive
> I'm well

I survive
I survive well.

The eight women say in unison:

We will rest together on our ambivalences.
We will share islands
as we struggle
toward an uncharted shore.

(The eight women carry their pillows off the stage.)

End of Act One

Act Two

Act Two

SCENE I

Women Who Can't Rest On Their Ambivalences

(Note: This scene consists of four short vignettes with each set of characters entering and exiting from the stage. Should the theater have spotlights, and the stage be large enough, the stage may be pre-set for these episodes, with the actresses in place, and the lights turned on the appropriate spots when each vignette is enacted. There are no props for thin and fat self. There is a glass and bar stool for the second vignette, two chairs for the psychiatrist's scene and a bench for the jail cell. Suitable substitutions or additions may, of course, be made, such as a large mirror for thin and fat self.)

Vignette One: Thin Self And Fat Self

(Two women enter, both the same age, same hairdo and color hair, but one thin, one fat.)

(Holding hands, facing audience, they recite in unison the following:)

> Not all of us can rest on our ambivalences.
> Our ambivalences make us restless.

Two lunches
one lean
one rich
one for thin me
one for fat me.

Which is real me?
Which is good me?
Which is bad me?
Which shall I be:
this year
next year
always?

How boring
It must be
to be
in the same flesh
forever.

I can be
she or me
fleet seductress
or slow sweet
earth mother.
We have more clothes
or disguises
than anyone.
Thin me
in baby blue
and pink.
Fat me
in black and blue.

Two lunches
two wardrobes
two lives
two selves
two cages
too much
too bad
too sad.

The world
does not know
who I am
nor do I really
know which
is me.

We have been
every size.
We know how
everyone feels.
We are
everyone.

(Fat self pulls away her hand angrily and facing thin self says:)

This twin-ing bores me.

There you are
clothed in your thinness
elegance understated
by my over-stated presence
socially berated
and self hated

with audience deceived
by my laughter.

Fat me
seems big and powerful.
Outside a threat
but weak from tears
unshed.

THIN SELF: Thin me asserts
appears, allows
accepts applause.

Thin me, though outside
self-confident,
efficiency personified,
can be destroyed
by the slightest threat.
Then she hides
in the fat woman.

FAT SELF: Fat me resents
returns, reminds
reclaims, re-enacts
retreats.

Fat me has
seized a large space
in this world
but has not
filled her emptiness.
For griefs and injuries
she takes candy bars

ice cream, loaves of bread
chewing anger.

Where but inward
can her anger go?
Like an armadillo's armor
she layers pain
upon her body
making her body
a fortress.

Nothing shall reach
her there
or tempt her out.

THIN SELF: The tense cheekbones know
the aching jaw knows
the thumping heart knows
the tight breath knows
the rising fluids know
what mind and mouth deny.

That fat woman
is going to kill me
unless I kill her first.
Which will it be
she or me?

Can I reason with her?
Can she remember?

Coming out of fat
I find a forgotten self

in my closet
light, lithe dresses.

Coming out of fat
I salute the mirror
an old friend.
The moat collapses
around a weighty enemy
suddenly a strangèr.

Coming out of fat
I run the stairs
with breath to spare
and dream of dashing
through open fields
to celebrate Spring.

FAT SELF: That's easy when you're not depressed.

Do you know what depression is?

It crawls out of bed with you
grayer than the darkest morning.
Even three cups of hot coffee
and the warm, scented bath
cannot shake the chill.

Wherever you may go or run,
it goes along, unwelcomed.
Reject it, but it shares your day,
your friends, your food and work,
its voice louder in stillness
but heard above all distractions.

There are those blessed times
when finally untwined and free
you celebrate your gratitude
incredulous the parasite persisted
determined never to host it again
and all the angrier when
the twin returns to share again
your bed, your day, your strength.

THIN SELF: You sound desperate.

FAT SELF: I am.

Having more hope
or responsibility
or lacking the courage
of Sylvia Plath
or Anne Sexton
I kill myself
in increments
inches of obesity
strangling heart,
self-esteem
and womanhood.

Running always
yet almost unable to move,
I move to food
seeking and denying life
in one gesture
of anger and supplication.

The consumed consumes.

Too much demanded
too little returned.
I will take mine
even unto sickness
monstrosity and death.

THIN SELF: You have one litany you repeat like a frog's croak. In fact, I think you have a frog fetish:

You bought frogs,
indoor frogs,
outdoor frogs
frogs for your bath
and the birdbath
a kitchen frog
and a frog
signalling
in your window.
Even your daughter
bought you a frog
at rest.

Was it that
bloated beyond
recognition,
you are sister
to the frogs
or rather
that you desire
a frog prince
to rescue you
although
you know

fairytales
are for the young
and foolish?

(The two rejoin hands and recite in unison.)

Sometimes I wish
I could destroy
one me
or both
in one long binge
of lake water.

Well me
sick me
live me
dead me
which she
will it be?

Two lunches
one for thin me
one for fat me
which is real me
which is good me
which is really me
which shall I be
this year
next year
always?

(Arms linked, Thin and Fat Self leave the stage.)

Vignette Two: In a Bar

(Helene enters carrying a bar stool and sits on it. She holds a glass. Mary enters, and looks at her for a minute.)

MARY: It is ironic. Helene was voted most likely to
                      succeed by our class but when she came to the
                      25th reunion she was a mess. She was one of
                      the first of us to marry but her successful,
                      brilliant husband turned out to be a mean
                      bastard and alternated between abusing and
                      ignoring her and the kids. She is still with him
                      but their marriage is rotten. As for Helene:

                      Voice husky
                      from gin and tobacco
                      my girlhood friend
                      sits across the room
                      telling of troubles
                      unbearable and
                      borne in bars.

                      Wherever we go
                      she must pause
                      for a drink.
                      Her smoke combines
                      with my tears
                      so that I can
                      barely see her
                      and wonder,
                      not without anger,
                      if she I loved
                      is still inside.

I try hard
not to hate
this now stranger
destroyed by life
and by her remedies.

HELENE: *(lights a cigarette)*

We walking wounded
triaged to ourselves
barely visible
living alone
or with cats
or catastrophic people
are humans too.

Oh, I have sought
belongingness
but nowhere
have I found a home
except these bars
where I buy a seat.
Those who do not belong
long for companionship.
Even Thoreau left Walden.

Full circle
I come
from loneliness and pain
to this circle my glass
and doubled pain.

Life which withheld
may yet give
and so can be trusted.
Life which destroyed
is a buzzard.
One runs from buzzards
or your flesh is theirs.

(Helene holds up a glass.)

Peter, who is to say
I do not love you well
because another lover
wooed and won?

MARY:

Too many yesterdays
creep into todays.
Her clock is clogged
with soggy memories
unresolved and
unresolvable.

Her clock threatens
to stop
and she to stop it.
She who raced
against time
is running
out of time.

(Mary leaves the stage.)

(Helene drains her glass and slowly weaves off the stage.)

Vignette Three: Psychiatrist's Office

(A woman in a white physician's coat enters followed by Catherine, about 50. The psychiatrist puts two chairs on the stage and sits on one and motions to Catherine to sit on the other. Catherine huddles in the chair slumped over, very still and withdrawn. The psychiatrist reads from her notebook as if reading a case report to herself.)

PSYCHIATRIST:

Battered enough
she braced
for another blow
and when
it did not come
remained frozen
waiting.

Let me review the case history. She was referred to me by her internist because she kept getting physical symptoms with no organic cause. She was brought up like many women of her generation to be good and to be a lady under all circumstances.

She drank the draft diluted.
Emotions too were muted
in patterns primly suited
to lull each living note.

She walked in paths soft lighted
and passion's fire was slighted
for fear her heart once sighted
would rising sear her throat.

She said she was contented.
Beneath, her pain fermented
as heart and soul resented
her holding life remote.

(Turns to Catherine.)

How are you feeling, Catherine?

CATHERINE: Like walking alone
                    in November
                    on rotted oak leaves
                    in cold rain
                    at midnight
                    knowing winter
                    will close
                    you in soon
                    and forever.

PSYCHIATRIST: That bad!

CATHERINE: They will find me there
                    in my unclean house
                    by the stink of my rot
                    wafted through closed doors
                    and bolted windows.

PSYCHIATRIST: I am sorry you feel so terrible.

CATHERINE: My parents told me
                    not to cry.
                    You said I could.
                    I cry now

for pains frozen
a half century.

I walk across
the bridge to Tuesdays
where I have a life
within a life
that turns reality
to drama mused upon
with you who I beg
to love me a little
or pretend you do.
Let me love you
in a life within
a life of shadow.

PSYCHIATRIST: I know I have become important to you in our time together. I do care. But you need to make a life in the real world.

CATHERINE: Nests are hard to come by
and fledgling fliers

often fall
to unreceptive ground.

Full grown, I staggered frozen to your doorstep where warm, protected from the storm outside, I dared the storm within – seeing in your eyes unfaltering stars and in your hands barriers against that fatal, final misstep into the chasm always underfoot and calling.

To leave the doorstep of an imperfect mother
with only young fears is hard enough. To leave
the doorstep of a perfect mother with adult
knowledge of the raging storms is too much to
ask.

> I do not trust life or myself, only you.
> I cry, "stay with me always; I am afraid."
> But you offer me a paradox.
> To earn your approval and my own
> I must give you up.
> I have to learn to conjugate
> the verb to be
> in the first person singular
> and the present tense.

PSYCHIATRIST: That's right. You have to work on your life in
the world outside this office. You have a lot to
offer in the real world.

CATHERINE:

> I shall be free as you would have me free
> and armed enough to bear the pain of
> parting and leaving you, go on with hope
> to see this present tense
> of life now starting.

> Though now I stand against the door
> reliving history once more
> please know I will not drag your light
> into the grave where I have lived so long.

> Please wait until I feel by day and night
> that I am I for once and I am strong.

PSYCHIATRIST: I understand what you are asking me so movingly. But unfortunately we do have to deal with reality, even here. You have more strength than you know. I am sorry but your health insurance is used up for psychiatric treatment. I know you cannot afford the fees I have to charge because of my realities. The next session will have to be our last. We will talk then about how you will manage. I will give you a list of self help groups in the area and also of social agencies which have low fees. We will say a proper goodbye. Now our hour is up, regretfully. I hate to push you out but another patient is waiting.

CATHERINE: Thank you.

PSYCHIATRIST: *(gets up and walks to edge of stage.)*

That was painful. I'm exhausted. I hated doing that. But I can't work for nothing. I must support myself. I tried hard. She's better than when she came. At least I haven't made her drug-dependent. She feels better physically. Before, she was headed for unnecessary surgery. She could have used more therapy. But there are so many others waiting, so many casualties. They keep slipping on the ice, and there seems to be nobody out there sanding the streets.

I have needs too. Patients expect more of women doctors and I suppose of other women professionals. And they get angrier at women than at men when we can't deliver everything forever. The Catherines see us as perpetual nurturers but we are only human.

Each woman's
pregnant face
invites
seduction
rejection
always.

My breast is empty
My ear is tired.
Please take
endless troubles
other places.
Help yourself.
Be quiet.
Manage.

For now
I am out of
chicken soup
and the only client
for my couch
is me.

(Psychiatrist leaves the stage quickly.)

(Catherine leaves the stage slowly.)

Vignette Four: In Jail

(Enter Sara, Consuelo, Lois, Beth and Sister Mary Caritas. They wear peace buttons. They sit on a bench.)

SARA:

They want us to post bail and get out of here but we won't. They put us in jail for protesting the missiles and we'll stay here to make people aware.

CONSUELO:

Yes we must do what we can to stop a war. We'll stay.

LOIS:

Agreed. But the dirt in this cell is awful and I need a bath.

BETH:

Agreed. But it is very annoying to have those guards keep yelling dyke. It is also maddening that the newspapers keep diverting attention from our anti-war protest to snicker than I am a lesbian. They don't bother mentioning that

you, Sara, are married, and you, Lois, have a male lover and Consuelo is a widow.

SARA:

Beth, you forget they keep writing about my kids being at home unmothered while I am here in jail. They forget the kids have a father. The truth is they don't see women at all as full people. They trivialize the causes we believe in and don't take our political actions seriously. They simply point to our sexuality, whether heterosexual or homosexual, and to our mother role as if that is our only identity.

BETH: You're right.

LOIS: To tell the truth, when they don't take us seriously, even I, sometimes, in weak moments, begin to wonder why we put ourselves on the line for a cause that is probably lost anyway. They keep building the weapons and starting wars no matter what we do.

SARA: I think we'd better remind ourselves why we are here.

CONSUELO: That would be good.

SISTER CARITAS: It would help me also to seek why we are here. The bishop's lawyer wanted to pay a fine and release me. I want to come to the truth of it. Was I wrong to do what I did and to stay here?

BETH: Okay, let's talk about it. You first, Sara.
SARA: It may sound dramatic when I tell you how I feel but I feel that way.

A life needs goals to stretch toward.
I saw in my children's soft young faces
my mission and my goal.
I would give them love
and the world would be theirs.

I kissed each warm and precious cheek
but when I recognized
what the world really is,
I pulled away in shock
to find the death heads cold beneath.

I saw my Jewish children's children
marching to the gas ovens
all bringing with them little goals
like worn out toys to bed.

I also saw that
as we stockpile neutron bombs
which destroy only life, not property,
children stroll slowly home from school
through radioactive rain
carrying mutated, defective genes
clutching schoolbooks celebrating war
yearning for uniforms and guns
holding already congealed concepts
of we and they – properly socialized
made too stupid to love.

During Vietnam and the Gulf War
our children
burnt villages, burnt flesh.

The generals tell us
international relations
are too complex for us.
It is hard even to remember the names
that separate us into nationhood.

But I know we shall have peace
only if we wish it enough.

Mothers have a special responsibility to work for peace. That is why I am here.

LOIS: It's interesting that you, a Jew, and I, a Christian, are close in values. Some of the things you just said could have been written by a person who inspired me, Dr. Albert Schweitzer. He was a Christian clergyman, physician and winner of the Nobel peace prize many years ago.

He said, "the spirit is a mighty force for transforming things." He also said, "we shall have peace only when we want peace" and have "reverence for life" and "rediscover the fact that we all together are human beings."

Some of us awakened even before Vietnam or the Gulf War. My revulsion for war started during World War II.

As a young Red Cross volunteer
I walked daily through trains
of three-tiered stretchers
with mutilated men, my age then,
glad to leave the killings
but never young again.
I also walked through trains
of caskets.
I walk there still.

Later, after Vietnam,
my student veterans
wept to me their despair and guilt.
It was our guilt too.

In this time of fatal irreverence for life, this Christian joins with you, Sara, a Jew. We both belong to what Schweitzer called "the fellowship of those who bear the mark of pain." He meant by that those who have felt hurt, can empathize with hurt, help to heal hurt and end the hurting. That is why I am here.

BETH: I suppose I am anti-war
because I am a physician
I have glimpsed the wonders
of the cell and human body
so marvelous and beautiful
that even brilliant scientists
aren't sure how it all works.
But a bullet can stop life instantly.
Lungs are a marvel of design
but fallout destroys a million lungs.
Our Gulf War veterans are ill
from the poisons.

Between the wars
they mourn the dead
and hide the wounded
and speak of peace
meanwhile arming.

You know, one semester while in medical school, during the winter break, I went to St. Augustine, Florida. There is an old fort there, the Fort of San Marco, which is beautiful. It's right on the bay. Ferns grow in the furnaces which were used in colonial times to heat cannonballs to set enemy ships afire. Now, people sit peacefully on the walls enjoying the beauty of the old walls, the birds and water. It is a tamed fort. My dream is that all the energy that goes into war preparation and war itself can be channeled into preserving and enhancing life. As a physician, my job is to conserve life and nuclear war may destroy it utterly. That is why I am here. Sister, why are you here?

SISTER CARITAS: Well, you all know that the work our Lord gave me to do was to run a city kitchen that feeds those no one else will feed. Lately, with the high unemployment, we have had so many more people coming – including fine proud people. They are ashamed because they can't get work though it is not their fault. People of all religions and kinds ask us for all types of help besides food because many government and government subsidized social services have been cut or eliminated. The government is spending our money on arming itself and other countries. I needed to come to the truth of why such a rich country can not take care of its own people and why countries all over the world are impoverishing their people also to stockpile armaments when indeed there are enough munitions now to destroy civilization.

I prayed and prayed to understand and for help for the world. Then one day during Mass I felt God wanted women to say the time had come to end war and preparation for war. So I joined you on the picket line. And when they told us to leave, I stayed with you. And when they dragged you to the police van, I refused to move also. So they took me to the van too. I noticed that they carried me gently though, and I prayed for you who were being handled roughly. I pray also for those Nuns, Sisters of mine in Christ, who have been killed and suffered abominations for their work against war and for the people.

CONSUELO: Thank you for your prayers, Sister. I guess it is my time to tell why I am here. I will not say it as well as you who have more education. I had to go to work very early and worked all my life in factories, even when my children were small. There was not time for books. My husband did hard labor. He died young, worn out. My children are grown now and I have only myself to take care of but I feel I must have care for the world.

There has not been much work in my city lately. The shoe factory where I worked for twenty years closed. The only job I could get was making parts for the bombers that America supplies other countries to use in their wars and that our government buys to prepare for war. I didn't like doing this work but I had to eat and pay my rent and help my neighbors.

I've always been a hard worker and last month they decided to give me twenty cents extra an hour because I was so fast. Can you imagine twenty cents when the company makes so much money on those government contracts? Anyway, one night I saw on television the dead and terribly wounded people after a bombing raid. Some looked like my children. I couldn't eat, I couldn't sleep. The next day I told my boss to keep the twenty cents extra an hour and the job. I would not anymore make weapons to kill people. I took a bus to your city hoping to find work that was not bloody. I happened to pick up one of your anti-war leaflets on the street. I must do what I must do to face myself. I love this country but not what it is doing now.

LOIS: It was good to share. I feel better, reinforced.

(Sara, Lois, Consuelo, Beth and Sister Caritas stand and recite together:)

We are in the middle of
war and peace,
radicalism and conservatism
private concern and political action
activism and retreatism

convenience and the environment
our country and universality.

We WILL MAKE SPLASHES
as we thrust
with other women
toward a shore uncharted
but not denied
by us.

(End of Vignette Four and end of Scene One, Act Two.)

SCENE II

Questioning and Celebrating

(The entire cast comes onto the stage and the small groups who have been in scenes together sit in separate clusters. As each person speaks, she stands and when through speaking, sits again.)

MARY:

> Strong trees break
> when the storm hits hard,
> Why do I go on
> waving the branches
> like a fool or a beckoner?

LISA:

> Those of us going into marriages
> and those of us coming out of marriages
> pause as we pass, asking
> why such strains?
>
> Those of us going into jobs
> and those of us coming out of jobs
> look each other in the eyes
> with deep compassion.

JENNIFER: Who shall protect us
                   from these spiders
                   these managers
                   these leaders
                   who spin papers and words
                   in such corrupt webs?
ALICE: Where shall we go
                   to dream those dreams
                   to keep us from the sewers
                   and the grave?

LOIS: Why do most jobs
                   why do many marriages
                   alienate men and women
                   from each other
                   and themselves?

ELLEN: I don't know. I only know that:
                   I came into this isolation
                   knowing that before we parted
                   we lay body to body
                   man and woman together
                   unclothed and unmasked
                   in our need for comfort
                   yet could take none from each other
                   for more than a moment –
                   a moment I recall weeping
                   for what might have
                   strengthened us
                   instead of sending us
                   to weep alone.

Why, when life is loss
and humans fragile,
don't we cling together
instead of blaming those
we love the most?

How can we revenge ourselves
upon the world
instead of upon each other
or ourselves?

LISA: It's so sad.
                 Somewhere
                 someone
                 somehow
                 something
                 soon
                 please.

SARA: The somewhere is here.
                 The someone is ourselves, sisters.
                 The somehow is direct action.
                 The something is unity.
                 The soon is now.

                 There is no time for waiting
                 No strength to spend on tears.
                 There is no place for forgetting
                 or seeking escape from the world.
                 We can't shield ourselves.
                 We must wield power
                 Now is our hour.

ELIZABETH: I admire you, Sara, but women don't have much power now. Not all of us are able or ready to go to jail for our convictions. Some of us take care of the everyday. I take care of my ninety-four year old mother who is frail in body and mind. Nobody else will do it. Women help as they can. Look at Dora:

> She knows
> where to find
> hope, strategies
> diversions
> and even laughter.
> Dora connects us
> to herself
> and each other.

DORA: Yes, I believe we are all connected, men and women and nature. In my life, I have seen how people have lost sight of that.

RUTH: Nature is important to me. Though my grandmother and mother lived in slums, they taught me to love the earth. In the crowded, dirty city, we always had plants blooming in the windows and on the fire escape. Strangers would wonder how mother and grandmother made so much light in tiny dark spaces. They didn't know they did it through love and a need to foster growth.

Marmita even stole for her plants. Our neighborhood had only cement and gravel.

Marmita would have thought it funny that people now buy dirt in stores, what we call potting soil. She went to the park with a bag she sewed from a worn out coat and dug up loam from behind the rose bushes. "They won't miss it," she said.

Jane's dream was that someday she would have a farm in the country. Well, she never got her farm. But on summer nights she took me up to the roof of our apartment house and showed me the skies.

I have always loved the moon. I remember, as an adolescent during World War II, being shocked to hear on the radio that there had been a successful bombing raid in those pre-radar days because the moonlight allowed pinpointing the targets.

Up until then, for me and many people, the moon had been a symbol of tranquility, peace, love, and womanhood. Well, then men landed on the moon and now the moon is a symbol of the space age which makes possible terrible weapons.

I think women should reclaim the moon. If you wouldn't think it silly, we could all come together in a circle and I could recite my womanchant about the full moon.

(The women link hands in a circle.)

RUTH: Moon lit
moon struck
we gather
to celebrate
the full moon
in this full circle
our own
full moon.

We are moons
round
cyclic
constant
givers of light
sewers of buttons
fillers of cups.
We women
know circles.

We come
in ones and twos
and groups
for respite
share beauty
dreams, laughter
hopes
sorrows
tensions
fears
and in the sharing
gain courage
for another month.
For another struggle.

                                Full moon
                                full hearts
                                full house
                                full cups
                                full friends
                                full wombs
                                for some
                                full joy.

RUTH: Speak who you are.

(Each actress gives her real name and then says daughter of and gives her mother's name and then says granddaughter of and gives her grandmothers' names.)

RUTH: Moon lit
                                moon struck
                                we gather
                                to celebrate
                                the full moon
                                in this full circle
                                our own
                                full moon
                                of women.

                                The world is a circle
                                it is our circle
                                our only circle
                                everyone's circle.

                                Speak of this
                                to those daughters and sons
                                who will follow.

DORA: Let's come closer together.

(The women come into a tight cluster. As they do, they raise their voices in laughter, in joy, in sorrow, in anger, in hope, in pain, in various words and tones, until the sound is overwhelming. They embrace.)

The End

Author's Note:

If discussion is desired, the leader might start the discussion by saying, "You are part of this poetic drama of women's voices. Are you in the middle? Are you in between? Who controls the tides? Do you rest on your ambivalences? Will you make splashes? Now it is your turn to talk about any feelings, thoughts, disagreements or anything else the play aroused in you."

The discussion leader should give the audience time and freedom to react rather than asking very specific questions as the reaction will vary according to the composition and needs of the audience.

The author would be grateful for any reports of audience comments or reactions or for suggested changes or additions to the play. See her address at the beginning about Performances and Royalties.

Book Title	Qty	Price	Total
Be An Outrageous Older Woman		$14.95	
Button, Button, Who Has the Button		$12.00	
We Speak for Peace		$14.00	
Women Who Touched My Life		$14.95	
Merchandise	*Qty*	*Size*	*Price*
Outrageous T-shirt (Pink on Purple) (Sizes S, M, L, XL, XXL, XXXL)			$15
CT Residents Add 6% Tax			
Shipping—$3.50 First Item, $.50 Each Addtn'l Item			
TOTAL (Checks on US Bank or Money Order)			